Why We Go To Zoos

poems by Noah Leznoff

INSOMNIAC PRESS

Edited by Mike O'Connor
Copy edited by Sandra Dawson & Liz Thorpe
Designed by Mike O'Connor

Canadian Cataloguing in Publication Data

Leznoff, Noah, 1959-
        Why we go to zoos

Poems.
ISBN 1-895837-03-0

I. Title. 23|2|99

PS8573.E996W49 1997	C811'.54	C96-932449-9
PR9199.3.L49W49 1997		

Printed and bound in Canada

Insomniac Press
378 Delaware Ave.
Toronto, Ontario, Canada, M6H 2T8

Acknowledgements:

Some of the poems in this book, or versions of them, first appeared (or will appear) in:

Blood and Aphorisms ("Joe's Holiday"), Hook & Ladder ("Free Poem" and "Performance Anxiety"), Jones Av. ("eschatology," "Dancing for the Boy Next Door" and "Supermarket Lobster Story"), The Literary Review of Canada ("Barbara, Dental Hygienist", "Saturday Walking" and "Scissors, Rock, Paper")MuseLetters ("repairman to his royal"), Oversions ("It was Clean and Good") The Sandburg-Livesay Anthology ("the wind is blowing me away!"), Quarry ("Tit Mountain" and "In Moonlight After Rain") and Vintage '96 ("Face painting for Helen").

"Why We Go To Zoos," "Text as Amphetamine," "Girl or Cat" and "A Philistine Reads the Literary Supplement" were first published in Mad Angels and Amphetamines (Insomniac Press, 1994).

For their patience, fresh eyes and candour, the author thanks: Elizabeth O'Brien, Steve Manners, Stuart Pickford, Peggy Nadel, Paul Murray, Doug Heaman, Diana Bryden, and Mike.

I. Headland

II. The Variance of Bone and Bleb

III. Scissors, Rock, Paper

For Liz, Hannah and Chloe

Headland

If in my human arrogance I claim to read
her eyes, I find there only my own animal thoughts:
that creatures must find each other for bodily comfort,
that the voices of the psyche drive through the flesh
further than the dense brain could have foretold,
that the planetary nights are growing cold for those
on the same journey who want to touch
one creature-traveller clear to the end...

Adrienne Rich, from The Dream of a Common Language

Face Painting For Helen

I think I know
why some women go nuts
for make-up —

it's the little bottles and jars
 they like, the thick glass,
the caps, ramekins,
 plastic hinges;
it's those diminutive
 clamshell clickings and tiny
brushes
   nested, it's the
 protractions & retractions
(neat paraphernalia, like
   the drug-user's)
 and the mirrors
that show them them-
selves piece
by piece,

disclose
 each detail — slide
of colour,
 the variance of bone
and bleb

 But for me standing
clean-shaven now
with the cruses and tubes
you've left
 the first seduction is
simpler, infinitely, than eyes
 or skin: it's

 the weighted turn of design in
the hand and cut/of vitreous
stone: it's those little
 bottles

And

    singing my skin
and singing sad and joyous
implying goodbye to this and that
I joked with a stray dog

he'd come wagging
his star-thick tongue, wiping
firmaments on my hand,
his tail a baton

for a time
we marched sideways together

girl or cat

   a girl, about thirteen,
      sits on the roof
      of a summer car

  her white hand like a beak
dangles a cloth, with slow swirls
   dripping, metal glinting, barely
   touching

    (she is humming)

Why We Go to Zoos

So I'm at MarineLand, Sea World,
some oxymoron of place, having
come down
the quiet stairs to watch the
two white whales from underneath,
and the crowd's a dark conundrum
of shadow before the turquoise
glass — beanpoles, I discern now,
elbows in safari shorts clicking
Pentaxes like there's no
tomorrow, wide hard women
wiping kids who drip sugar
cream from their hands
and chins,
and these belugas, these
mother fucking big fish,
are passing back and forth in
front of us. And
they're all white muscle,
all soft marble, smooth rubber,
and I want to touch them
like horses,
and their foreheads
are square and quizzical and their
eyelids have human
wrinkles,
and,
I swear,
they're grinning. Like they know
they're ostensible mythologies
or something.

But some... other colour,
a curlicue, tendril,
worming from the integument, flap,
then more and more to a fully protracted
 (holy shit) hooked fleshtone
dick flubbering through the water,
a viscid, shaggy animal
 in its own right,
   thin gel rinsing from
it like heat rippling
   the air. And the big
grin sweeps wide and
bumps her, straining
to roll her, throwing
with everything:
spine, tail,
flanks ivory and hard,
a pounding like no grace
   on earth.

 I'm thinking *Holy fuck...*
'cause the whales alone are
enough, but now they're almost
screwing inches from my nose; the female's
so white and big, turning
pressed against the glass so close I can lick her;
the male's rubbing into
her, working to nudge
   under her tailside
and she's wriggling
her goddess backside, shaking her cetaceous
booty, rolling
like a cloud,
and she's beautiful and white
and she's taut and smooth and white,

smiling hard against the glass
and an elbow's jabbing hard
into my ribs, Liz is hitting me
'cause now I'm shouting HOLEE FUCK!
at the top of my lungs and this sudden
silence and echo
and the lens-heads are shushing
their kids the hell
out of there or fumbling with film
canisters, and the glass might break,
and the cock is slippery and grinning
and she cuts at the last
second, glides to the far
blue wall, circling

and the cock, the cock is after her
and the cock jazz shivering through the water
and the cock much bigger than my own
(no less pink, cock-serious) and
the male's eyes serious
and against her his whole musculature's
quivering like a
leaf.

Supermarket Lobster Story

From eight feet away
i imagine it whooping, transfixed
as i am in some Jungian aspic, some bright
crustacean tongue or if, or however,
those things make sounds of joy

Like a kid all morning up
and down a slide,
back and forth, this flying lobster
this lobster pawing the lip
this celebrant lobster letting go, straddling
the aerated jet
  riding the ride
then breast-stroking it back
to the mouth of copper tube

Again, there he flies: *Ayyeeeeeeeeeee!*

i break from the instant cheese
 section, full
of stupid love for this:
   sensation
a rush under the carapace
wild wind on the underbelly, even
   here

where his fellows lie inert,
black and green, piled high like
centurions or strata of dead
geology

Much closer, of course:

They've had their antennae snipped. I've known
all along of the fat blue rubber bands
that clamp their pincers like the ribbons
that once bound the feet of Chinese
princesses,

but this antenna trick makes everything dizzy

and Billy Bishop's been clipped to the bridge;
  three legs on his right side, chewed
and mangled, half-hang like broken straw

and it's no primitive joy lifting him
  back to the nozzle each time
but the tank's clockwise breathing

circadian

 wake slowly
from bedrock,
fumble wet the
white currant jam,
drip into your suit
as off a slow spoon

like a crow in a tree
 stand in the open doorway,

 smell a shoulder of rainy weather,
wait naked in the naked branches

then drive the oiled road,
wakes of charred stalk field,
stubble beards, holding
your chatterbox with two hands
under a sheet-metal sky

 you hear radio
from this metal, numbered deaths
 in the same steady voice

 not-
withstanding the autumn rain,

 wipers flapping like sea-
birds lifting
      from still water

Text as Amphetamine

After I said, "Come in"
Hal stood there looking jumpy as hell,
purple-black smudges around his eye sockets,
nervous hands and posture, white as the moon.
It was three a.m.

In another incarnation he was beautiful,
a junior golfer, sun glinting from his V-neck:
Been tripping for thirty-six straight, he
told me, and his teeth swung in his mouth.

Under his arm, a pretty girl, compact, also blonde
who he introduced as "Sheila, a kindergarten
teacher." I tried to imagine her with children,
and it fit,
except for the grim reaper beside her and the fact
that it was a school night.

Morning, really.
Steve was not home because the Cubans were after him.

That afternoon I'd found a note in the kitchen:
"The Q's are after me. You don't know
where I am." Which was true.

The golfer and kindergarten teacher made
small crazy talk before
the door closed behind them.

I heard the car's slamming, the engine-gun,
a shifting to smaller and smaller noise.

Everything was quiet again; it was black outside.

I continued to read.

Dancing for the Boy Next Door

You watch frozen as I
unhinge the fall of hair from my scalp,

fold it like a perfect cloth
over the chair-back.

Already my eyebrows, peeled
from the forehead milk, curl

like leeches on the dresser-top
— seconds ago my clip-on teeth

spread clattering there, clay beads
from an open hand.

You watch me stretch from the torso,
unzip a rib, disrobe shoulders,

wriggle from my girded hips as from
a vase.

The muscle and flesh come easily, lift
like fillets under my airborne fingers.

The Obvious

I've heard or read
about how ideas die:

it's not that one argument (so
the argument goes) convinces another,
or that the running tally
leaves one God foolish
while the other grins
or pulls a moon,

or that some currency bullies
its rival to paper

but rather old words sit
in bone furniture
until history dissolves them

On the other hand,
I've seen wisdom
beaten out of the young
or weak, beaten so deep
there is no underground

Saturday Walking

Walking the street
covered in simplicity like air
like rain-thick wind humming
and no nothing tired,
but a road moved healthily under me
and the wind made a sail of my shirt.

Balancing eyelids and dances, my fingertips
and fireflies, I watched the sunrise crash
against the continent — everything heaved;

I stretched my skin from sleep fetching
sticks for a stray dog.
It was that clear morning accumulation,

morning for leaving margins with blue veins
for receding houses and bric-a-brac,
for feet becoming heartbeats.

When a roadside redness gathered me in,
mistook my silence for its echo, the rooster
grasses for the wind blowing them warm,

I knelt to gravel and a stone lisped: *listen*—
and overhead, a thousand geese came honking; the sky
was a marble table, blue and grey; the clouds, women
playing in the white lake of the sun.

And lying lost on a path the dog and I watched
a yellowjacket glitter till its crying
died; and to that tremulous leaf that blew by
our nostrils spread like strange fish fanning,
and our tongues dug bowls in the earth
to mark where it fell and moved from.

What supped in my lungs, I wonder, when we stood inside my mouth?
It grew so cold and blue, made me throw my arms to pinwheels,
made me wrap my mountain skin in clover and dust,
and when I shivered out of my sleeve, shaking in the grass
like wind, and when the pond-lip suckled me like a leech,
a clean-licking fruit — that's when groundwater
broke, and our bodies shattered

Beehive

1.

And when he came back
he was another asshole wandering
though young men riddled his cheek
with derision

and when he came back
he was another underthing
holding his hat on his lap, smiling
for money, pretending he was king

and when he came back
the rich and foolish both in nets;
the dead wore tall black hats
were elegant

2.
The Wise Guys:

they were making, making, making thought
the pedant elbowed at the trough
enounced the multi-singular,
warm splashing the pot

this child is as dead as paper
he washed his face in ink

3.

Late January. the grass
is yellow as a colonel's beard
as corn is brushed by weather
small pompadours, cowlicks
the morning hair

4.
epigone

but he recognized on the nose of a
dog waiting to cross the street, looking
both ways, the imperative of training

5.
against erica's domestic anxieties and liniments
he conspired to construct degrees of love by phone
(he fell very short

6.
a tongue fumbled with the snap of her eyes
pop pop
he is handsome

moon cream
an indelicate discretion

7.
fools' moon, lyre and mandolin

8.
rooftops crept to every window
gables, periscope chimneys;
each day the neighbourhood waved closer
an orthodontic amity

9.
Two dogs were staked to a single post when the caribou stampeded.
Responsible citizens, they buried the eye teeth.

10.

      apart   a part

Tit Mountain, St-Donat, Quebec

I remember the altitude of
vision, the certain atmosphere,
a long road curling distant to a toy town.

Upon the rock we played fashion models
to a boy-sized cross (some Brother must
have placed it there); we brushed up to

it, teased with our shoulders,
tossed our hair, blew gaunt pouting
kisses over the iron arms.

We laughed giddy, hung coy and cruciform, took photos.
We were feminine.

Tit mountain:
        erect we stand on nipple left,
        sucking blue air amid scrub and flies

our mouths cold with wind, our bare-chested
blasphemies stretching open and woundless

Saint Max

Brother of wild-wing
beating, your blue skin burnt
to wind-light ash,
I would gather you in my arms
like a pile of leaves,
 shape a hillock to cover
in a blanket, to roll and unroll
on the ground

and   kneeling I'd unwrap you
scrub the red
from your elbows, from your
scalp smouldering and smelling
of potatoes;
I'd take the ember
cool it in my mouth, kiss
too the blisters rising in
your eyes and the black lips
praying for immolation

Yeah I'll douse you, gods'
  half-man, so he may sit
like a good brother
and between breakfasts of mute
benediction count
the gentle candles of
  his toes

Fisherman's Back Porch

— for Brother Luke

>   Conceding honesty
as slippery as need or god
a carp not to be hooked, its mouth
at its chin, a bottom feeder,

the fisherman (unthinking)
outrigs his tackle — second nature of leader,
line, and lure; the spinning silvery thing
a machination.

An old-handed thumbnail
measures depths with just a glance,
knows what might live under a lake-skin,
jiggles the line a little.

The barb is beside the point (of course)
behind it: night-ripped flesh,
unready ascent, a dark metal taken
in hungry confusion.

Some men are children in water;
others lean from rocky vantage
dangling the sophistry of worms.
But no one's twisted fins here:

we really only want to cuddle fish,
to take them to our sleeve, as loving friend,
and waltz them round the clerestory
cheek to reddening cheek.

The Variance of Bone and Bleb

Being human, we
each of us can bear no more than a particle
of pain that is not our own; the rest is rhetoric.

Alden Nowlan, from "Bobby Sands"

Jingle

The mind is a target
 an audience
 a vote
I buy the invasion
a bar of soap

I'm sebaceous, man
 ivory, wet
the more you rub me
the smaller I get

the smaller I get
the smaller I get
the more you rub me
the smaller I get

I met a woman, lovely in her bones...

An Unscheduled Break

is a small revolution,

    two minute drive
from where I'm paid to be,
with a hum of wet lilacs coming

from the radio
 and the hopping mad sparrows
(crazy shits — I've seen them
peck their dead, but not today)

chirping their round business;

they must know this is where I park
to steal a cigarette,
 slurp coffee from
a plastic lid

Yeah, steal: drink deep;

the time is theft,
though I'd gladly cough
back the $ 1.57

for this precise burning
 a plausible story
those splotches of red

that close-eyed,
counting down the minute,
I almost mentioned

Barbara, Dental Hygienist

"The workers in store 27 are the best in the whole fucking chain."
— graffiti inside a delivery truck

'Glad to know that
she takes my mouth
  so seriously,
that the leeches
fossillized six
millimetres
below the gumline
are the object of
  her loathing —
that she means business.

Still, I wonder
  (rubber-gloved knuckle
      pressing my lower
lip into my chin)
what keeps her
  (money yes, but more…)
  at it, scraping me of god
knows what:

    there — a year's
  worth lined
on a gauze patch
on her sleeve
… bloody larval things.

              Ok. Diligence
but three quarters of an hour
    a thousand vein constricting shreads later
I'm thinking: Barb, if I were

you I'd say *Good enough:*
the demon's dead, fire's out!

But no, still she's
  leaning into me
like a workman to a jackhammer,
like a poet to a rubber poem,
    shaking her tight-wrought hair.

Like no one else, like nothing
  perfunctory or mercenary
she cares for a time about
  my mouth;
foul-breathed kisses seem easy
compared to this.

        ˋ At the session's end
when Doctor Yu makes her appointed
appearance,
  pokes in and around
for a minute or two
(and most of the take)
    then praises the exhaustive
scaling,

Barbara, Dental Hygienist,
      lets slip
  a blush-blooming smile

and me too (after
the maintenance
  lecture) walking
to the car,
pulling winter through her
  air-clean bones.

Soundtrack To Kigali

"She overcame a terrible tragedy, but she made it to the top and she intends to stay there."
— *Ted Koppel, about somebody or other*

He is led to the dying
by circus star apparitions
square-dentured uncles
glitter bodies flying
from cannons, swinging from
trapezes, juggling cars & genitals & brains
 in the national fish basket
 (the exhausted working day)
juggling him to facility,
to wake up and begin again tomorrow
to come home to his living
room of decorative forgetting.
    Dig a dog a bone.

An american horror story, too, makes good
television:
            deaths to engage
 deaths informed by high-
angle aesthetics
voiced-over deaths to enlarge our
    hearts,
        these deaths made possible
by anodyne interruptions
which are) themselves
interruptions to (commercials for
fear and pity and helplessness.

The mother sobs in slow motion

the soundtrack weeps
the bodies lobbed into a common
rut are covered in
plastic or corrugation;

the garbage bag is kick-tuff, animal
 resistant; families decompose in his
   bowl of fruit, his sweater,
his discount fire-sale Korean shoes.

He rewinds this news too late.
Smoke plumes from the millinery.
The moon rises like a logo.

You can't stare 'em down, it's like a law

the big eyes of a supermarket
 baby — eyes, the oldest part
of the whole damn infant

Smoker's Reckoning

She kept her ashes in a jar
jars and jars upon a shelf
rows of shelves of jars of ashes
walls of rows of shelves of jars
and rooms of walls, and walls of houses
rows of walls of houses, jars
jars of houses, temples, cities,
jars of mountains, oceans, stars
roomless walls, floating ashes
she kept her ashes in a jar

Free Poem

I'm looking for the free poem
the one that catches light

not the one shuffling with its hands in
its pockets like a man out of work,
 not the one
     wire-sprung like a trap,
  not the death song nor the ghost
   that mopes — its
face a shrunken white heart.

  and no crossword
puzzle trick or mirror dancing
 footnote-tipsy courtesan
tossing his flounce in your face
   — and not the wood stump grain
  that whittled itself to
nothing,
the form that nagged without loving

I'm looking for the free poem, the be-poem

  may-be the poem that boarded a train with
nothing but a mouthful of chocolate,
  a cold beer in the windbreaker pocket
  half a dozen twenties
   a window seat

A Letter to Alice

I.

Dear Alice:

the morning comes slow but crisp for… well, us (you and me)…
a little cold and overcast in the eastern region, steely through
the window morning news. but held against rainy months,
rubber weather we've carried lately, this musty old sweaterfor
nostalgia sky, this patient joe sun fishing behind the cloud,
seems a gentle enough landing (and a sleepy dog in a hollow
log). and still wearing your slippers and fooling with your
rub-the-face trick.

your fingers insinu(inu)ated htemselves
into my face like so many loving
instrumentsthe bones remember shaping:
the embryo clear within
the womb, a white splinter nail
inside that worm, definite face
stretching out, finfingers separating,
 eyes within the blue head, soft-boiled,
and peeled pear shoulders to arms, hands
folded asin prayer, the umbilical
insect dragging its sac, white semen silk,
dripping albumen.

Conclusion: mammals owe the world to
eggs.

Two Men bore an egg across a field.
Two Women gave it heat to let it grow.

II.

To Introspectives   [title

marsupials,
mammals, oviparous flapping
lend me your phylogeny

I come to bury myself not praise you
in the world's un inhabitable cup, sunrise
oh oleo, oogonium, happy bear traps for breakfast;
pellets of buckshot, desperately blown news bundles
of wet paper stacked on the neat lawn

we hate the wide world because it takes more time than

the last literate American president
took to call the mystics from Alexandria

:but what other worlds are coming!
O O! What foreign intelligences!

III.

starve world federalist:

love and landscape
estuary and memory run deeper, adam,
than politics of reproduction

You can pretend to keep mountains in your head,
can swallow a legion of dead
Trotskyites or self-pitying poets
  ideas of them, in a jar
like a child swallows an oyster
(with her eyes closed)

so kiss goodnight, cracker: good nudes
and fellow campers

[after the fellow campers have rolled
themselves into each other's
sleeping bags like so many, like so many
foil-wrapped pantry snacks

the real work of the revolution begins

…in the corner of a back
room, house on a shoulder of the land
fire like a red mole on skin

   through a window
   a stone field across which

two women are walking

soldiers or lovers

sisters and tall swaying trees
agents of the lesbian nation of truth

lesbians who nurse children to power
broad-backed muscled-shirted lesbians who arm-
   wrestle my arrested dreams
lesbians who saw The Sound Of Music
and were moved to sing the living hills

or unspoken fisherwomen for the sea,
or Sunbathers for Amnesia

but no,
the women are proud and ardent: between sloppy wet-
beautiful kisses
they map a popular front, an education campaign
that is [revised in portfolio three] as follows:

IV.

Two lesbians stranded on a beach on TV
lesbian women and two gay men, watching their complements
from a distant paradox, but finding,
through the grace of our lord and saviour, a calculus
in the grand other: strange accoutrements flushed

by dapplings of strength, rude shaken
feathers baking in the sun,
the sinewy muscularity of it all, realizing, despite
the overhanging tree-fact, that... that politics aside...

PENultimately they stride their conviction
across the convention floor, all four of them,
tall and free and hetero as the dickens
and, shaking hands as if the war were over,
renounce the island as an Usher house or a bad call
at home plate.

V.

two women, shoulders slender, walk like shadow tigers
(like just plain women) with a typical low red sun over tall
swaying grasses

the pitch of wood flutes, mosquito fruit, automatic weapons,
what have you

But here, no here, the sun (the one and only lord) is hard on
the house next door;
this room becomes whiter by minutes, by minutes

this room becomes numerically explicit,
empirical,

irrefutable,
absoluteish;
and we are here, wearing threes and light metres, just me
and me
and you and you

(the other people are off listening to records; this is our
only chance, our private moment)

VI.

Millions of People Do It: Reading In Bed
Pornographic Magazines
Being and Maquillage, The Lumpen-Intelligenitalia

You hope to make meaning by singing to the children of the
local community, positioning their hands just so, giving them
hunger, addicting them to detail or foolish dreams or, if
nothing else, open-eyed rapture. The Sodom you create exists
only in the privacy of your own home. and in tax
supported public galleries. I'm outraged.

children will be emaciated through till Saturday
when the sale ends soon.
William will pay the GST.
I will lend credence to the continuity

to which anarchy must accede, like children to nightfall.
I will cradle the lost boy from self-hatred and brutality. As
free as necessary and no more: come home, Alice, she's a bitter
cunt. sweet dreams to make her kind, chocolate in her
mouth, a New Year's penny for her slumber

"but that's too easy," Alice said
and
    sang to herself or tore her breasts open in a fit of beauty

Rough Accounting

you keep lessons
somewhere
a ledger
of need or
absence,

columns
of standing ink,
red stone,
 Chinese
characters
in an illegible
history

at night
you hold me
like a bad debt,
  make of my
idiot cock
a feather or
war toy

Lunch Hour

The fashion now is dire and my daughter
wears it black and metal, as it must
be worn, without tenderness
  but I've seen her throw
sandwiches to the seagulls.

We are miles from water;
garbage brings these mendicants
  to the school yard. I have
never seen their young.

Kids toss alms in the spring air,
  watch birds steal
baloney from each other's beaks,

  imitate
    their shrieking flight —
cigarettes pressed between
    lips, jackets flapping,
           they dip and sheer.

  On a Southern beach I watched
  two men down a pelican with rocks,
then, a little giddy — they'd
    surprised themselves —,
  attempt mercy-killing by jumping on it.

        The elbow-drop
was from WWF Wrestling; I recognized
it only because the taller man
  called the play-
by-play.
The bird died quickly or slowly.

As a kid I dropped a minnow in a cup
of gasoline to study a thing dying,
to imagine dying.

Television wants to keep us young.
Cartoon cities explode.

The clouds scud full against a good colour.
Our troops are overseas. The children are feeding
scavengers and pretending to be them.

The Surgeon General

warns staring into space
is hazardous to your eyes,
may harm the baby or reduce
life expectancy

the surgeon general knows
reading into night may
disequilibrate brain fluids,
that text is an amphetamine (one
   word can get you sacked)

the surgeon general warms
your urine in a glass,

test issue, and the bottle
has no lip or nipple.

Wiping the honeymoon from your chin
please undress now.

Neat's Foot Oil

What happened to all them neats?

There's a refugee camp packed chock-
full of beaver, who holding their leather tails
conspire in sibilants, who, with prune-shrunken
flappings, plot our castration

— where geese with murderous grindings and clicks
of the tongue, wait on waiting lists for dialysis
machines, mothering, liverless, hissing
intimate accidents, dropping them papered from the wing

and featherless cousins too, honking unicycle
horns and paddling in spirals; and skinless mink,
shiny, stringy, musculate red and purple, who devour
in that first casual logic their young

and around and around inside the compound
fence, the grim footless neats, scuttling on their
rumps in the dirt for loose kernels of feed
or cigarette butts the guards have tossed — the neats
silent around the sterno-can, playing euchre,
watching the chemical blue flame

A Philistine Reads the Literary Supplement

— to a critic who fears post-modernism's 'anarchic present tense'

it's true: with one luetic squirt they'll curdle
the whole damn alphabet, unravel morphologies,
send spiralling from the Sun King's shoulders, like felled eagles,
the noblest subsumptions to the shit heap

you see: a hill of beans, sea of sweat
will swallow syllogism after syllogism;
with lima hearts, with hands as big as stones,
with flesh, with flame, they'll make wisdoms of their own
the same wise music silence makes of poets

Yes: power & light are tenuous playthings,
thin as the public ribbons you string and cut,
floodlight suns, pancake brass oratory,
little girls from X lost in a well, the belated
tears of feminized Fathers. They have no face for this pathos.

From broken bones green tendrils reach and curl;
their growing's susurrus as lovers' fingers
more electric than pornography or metaphysics
and their teeth are harder, too, than concentric
onion-heads, more luminous than light bulbs
that buzz buzz buzz and fit in the palm for crushing

On *The Order of the Solar Temple and the Advanced Centre for the Study of Higher Sciences*

He thought it might be
lonely flying to the sun
on the blood of the infant
anti-christ
(he thought it might
be lonely)
— this good-looking Belgian/
Swiss/French guy
in tight lapels,
Maserati, Conference of Rome
 dental work

— this delusionary
fucker-priest hooded in
smoke, medieval
feathered party masks
marine corps all-nighters
light shows, sing-alongs
Fourth Reich astrologies

They too, the thirty-nine, were loaded
urbane & well-educated
 when he placed them
face-down, feet
hubbed to a sun-spoked
circle, their heads
Glad-bagged to catch
the drugged brain
matter and
splinters of skull.

Forgive me
if I prefer my clerisy dull.

eschatology

come into the cave with a candle
come into the water with a hand-on-fire
the black lake opens its throat
to the opening of your hand and mouth

the serious man swallows water-striders;
the woman swallows darkness in her womb
inside that cave the bone bare splintering
to turn somersaults in the epilimnion

the soft hand falls asleep, the candle
jumps over the nimble boy, sparks scatter
the room, climb the white walls and faulted ceiling

the shoreline the man the spider sucked
into the candle flame
the path, the gravid hanging branches
sucked into the candle flame
the village dawn consumed, the village
woodlot, dale, mountainside temple with
its candles swallowed by the candle
by the candle the candle released
and the statues and the stars and the crust shore
of the continent in that burning

Scissors, Rock, Paper

Poetry must resist the poetic almost successfully.

— *Wallace Stevens*, misquoted *from* Adagia

Conversations with Luigi

Luigi Persicino is losing his mind
For want of love or height or friendship
For being the only son and nephew, the last
candle his parents kept with prayer and quiet work,
kept with weeping to make potent and audible.

In the fall, he took straight A's to university;
at Christmas he came home with half a mind.

Now he apologizes whenever we happen in the park
 which is getting too frequent for my comfort.
He's a guy I know

 leaves messages of awful silence
on my answering machine,
 nonsense contrivances that
need only talk.

"Did you know that the letter A used to be
the horns of an ox? And ox comes from
a Greek word meaning 'wet'. Semen. Call me back
if you didn't know that, okay?"

 The ribbon cuts off with a beep,
 blurts again another beep.
 Again call waiting. Luigi. Fuck.

(This then, I guess, is the crux of brotherhood,
 humanism, pathos: trying to be kind,
 or at least interested, then waking up
 to find a ringworm nested in your
 backside.

Or: this, then, is justice — hard labour
　for voyeurism's strange predation,
　the glib, distanced curiosity; I mean,
　flirting with the half-mad just to be
sure we haven't missed something.)

Anyways,
　I called back
　　let him rant, splatter
　some of that dizzy
phantasmagoria,
　tried too to nudge him
to social organization — a night course,
t'ai chi, square
　　dancing, but I ended up yelling:

　"WEEJ, SEE A DOCTOR! IF YOU HAD A BUSTED
FOOT... C'mon, I'll set it up, I'll
take you."

　"I'm starting a rock band" — he hadn't heard
a thing — "we'll go on tour. I'll be the singer. You
　can play the tambourine."

　"I didn't know you could sing."

　"I sing all the time in the shower. You should
see my hair now."

　　　　　He started
falsetto into Queen's *Bohemian
Rhapsody*; he sang the whole thing.

　"That's great. Hey, did I tell you?
I'm changing my number. I'm going unlisted."

"I know where you live."

"Shit you do."

"I do. I know where you live and I'm coming over to kiss you."

I held the receiver, waiting for a word.

The line went dead,
droned.

Performance Anxiety

"They make their nests of clay, one mouthful at a time."
— from The Wonder of Canadian Birds
or
"How you make love is how God will receive you."
— Rumi

making love i can't shut out the train
in my
  head:

  will she come, will she come?
  is she coming, will she come?
  will she come, is she coming, will she come?

or
  how will this make the next touch
occasion love, that more or less generous
  everything —

  a full salad of kisses seeming
to ride on this humming-
bird wing,
this distance-sustaining pendency
  through sugar-carrying wood
between trunk and
  flower; this red

heart whirring at eighty vibrations per second;
heart coming, ruby-throated, to slough its own name;
red heart a birdly engine or blooded machine

But Christ, we've been friend enough to beauty, you
and me, to friendship — take your hand from my

mouth, say it:
      talk is good
      empathy is good
      books and film good good
      humour, honesty, volleyball, food
      good good good good

  no, say it now diving into me
the flat of your hands against my chest,
we'll say it together
as laughter
 nothing makes love like rumba

the wind is blowing me away!

that's what we take turns yelling our arms spread running
across the field, my daughter and I,
the wind is blowing us away
though my feet plod
in the manner of a wooden-legged giant
in fairness to a three-year-old's chasing
so I may play and seem to run, arms
pin-wheeling, head back
  the movie "whoooaaa" rising above the field and
wind we chase each other on, save each other
from flying over
  like cilia of dandelion seed
and running
(the wind is blowing me away)
  against the tugging on my jacket: "Don't worry, Dada,
I'm saving you!"

Scissors, Rock, Paper

Since I've stopped worrying about
death nights have become
 less interesting, I sleep —
no, not *worrying*, not *death* either (in the
abstract) — my death, my being
dead,
 a dream I had as a kid in which
buildings and freeways planted
 themselves on my burial:
   I pounded against the coffin lid,
yelled mute into a foot
of earth —
                    traffic
  whizzed by, lovers copulated or left
each other letters, business
 continued.

Years later I wrote:

                 Made
       restless by a quiet chorus
       of shadow, the gaze of shapes,
       clock's tick or some neglected
       third-hour wind

       he rose skin-quick, muttering
       from the bed: "Can't sleep
       for the life of this…"

and so on, gloriously awake.

  Now I find it far   too easy
to imagine accidents falling
on the bodies of my
daughters. I

fling pebbles at cars
speeding through the
 neighbourhood; keep
clippings on the new
 American Right,
poisoned lakes,
holes in the sky,
sudden mass mobilizations
of capital; I turn
quickly from televised
dramas of irradiated four
year-olds, everything but
the bewildered eyes white
 and shrunken

 or police-
yellow ribbons and forests
where the half-clothed body
is found.   I break

daily, spill open and exhausted from
the joy of them;
daily I must kiss them each a hundred
times, enclose myself around them,
smell them,
lick them,
count their generous fingers
and snug them into their own beds with
 butterflies and monkeys.

 What then against the mass of night
on their small bodies? Fatigue,
 the basement,
a smouldering solitude and quiet
 pen tapping paper like
  a white cane?

Landing

"…my forehead is still red from the Queen's kiss"
— Robin Blaser

Again I walk unbuttoned, let in the three-legged cat,
stand back to watch the snow sweep across a far field
barren steppe, moonscape, ice-refracting star

O Galaxy, Love-Slackened Widow!
My beard and coat expose me: I wait, key
in hand with seven nights' standing,
a porchstep spaniel whose star-bit face
is roundness poised for the parting

...all unround round, jack:

the black again over your shoulder, slattern
toss of constellation, child-belly in distension,
hospital mud and rock, aggregate nothing

I'm red as a leg, a boot, a birthday boy
and must sooner freeze under your hoary skirt
than fiddle the march of saints

Still Life

I have called you night for dearth of sense or day,
I'm tripping tripping tripping to Bombay
Pulling no lip-song twirling no parade
Rilke's copper wiring in a beggar's tinsel vein

today consumes the desperate apple of me
the sun's paint's still, the shadow after me
which is nothing to any red or green food,
shrunken fruit, brown interlude

It was Clean and Good

It was clean and good and brachydactyly
and we loved it, loved it, practically,
but oo-cha sang the singing branches,
the homeless bird, the cinnamon patches

It was cold and dead and brachydactyly
and we wore our fingerless factory
but oo-cha swept the giant bird wing
the insect tree, the entirety

It was from a form, brachydactyly
where we drew our circles tactically
no red sweet simple and no rushing pulse:
a word-head spinning in the rectory house
reticular! spectacular! in the white white light
while oo-cha squealed the back-trapped mice

Land of a Million

"Such a quantitative increase eventually makes for qualitative change…"
— Northrop Frye

Crossing the border I couldn't believe
the sign: "Welcome To The Land of 1,000,000 Poets"
which meant, I figured from my Rand-McNally,
nearly one citizen in thirty. A *typo*,

    I blinked, angling my visor
 to the sun splintering white and
orange, when around the next twist
a shadow — a kid, his thumb up.
 Turns out he wrote "sort of light erotic ballads"
to women whose eyes he'd never meet but whose
bodies he'd summoned again and again until golden
with verses they became his. He seemed
sincere. We sang with the radio.

At the Voyageur stop I kept my ears pitched
to the ordinary hubbub — teenagers' booming laughter,
road-work men scraping plates, kids crying or running wild,
exasperated parents, sighs.
 But the waitress was touched (when I
leaned to her order pad, though, she flipped
it shut chiding: "All good things").

The graffiti in the crapper:
oh, some scatology and hatred, fear, but
other swirls too that suspended me in
a cello note, a purple Vedantic hum…

And later: at bus shelters, in doughnut shops
everywhere folk reading or scribbling
— against mall mirrors; cross-legged
in the park, squirrel bodies rabbinically curled
 foreheads intent and buried
or scanning the treeline.

Of the academic presses, when I found them,
some condescended, some raged;
 impossible now, weary, to tell
the poets from the age; while outside

in the pigeon-strutted square a parliament
of expatriates played chess; branches bent
to a pair of lovers who dropped their guns,
 argued openly, wept.

And globbing sun-silvered around her
 lips, water from a public fountain;
I mean a girl on tiptoe leaned
her mouth to it.

Joe's Holiday

It is true what they say about daughters, even before they can speak.

Joe watched her take the nipple, the wetness of it, how it had become something different and wonderful too, Anna's nipple, long like the end of a little finger, and the shininess of it, the thin milk dripping as the infant withdrew. And how she squirmed in his arms at first trying to suckle, then, as she nested to their cradling, curled inside and quiet against his fat chest. And the night he held her to his cheek and danced her to radio music, singing softly and breaking with sugary joy when she sang back, a definite new whimpering.

And Anna was beautiful too, keeping her square, hard beauty. But long hours and overworked blood left her often silent and inward, though perhaps there was something else to it.

Anyway, he would do the standard: unbutton her sleeper and blow farting sounds into her belly or under the fatness of her neck to make her laugh outright. He would lie on his back on the carpet and she would crawl on top of him; he would roll her from side to side, a little roughly, but making sure of the head with his big hands, and she would shriek with fear and excitement and tiny vertigo. And once, lying on his side with her, he said before he had a chance to call it back: "I am teaching you how a man loves."

Usually when she was difficult to console at bed time he soothed her with rocking and with his voice before lowering her into the crib, and then let her cry for ten minutes so that would be that. It was what the doctor said they should be doing now, being firm about bed time. But she had slept a lot today, or maybe was afraid of a new apprehension, or was thirsty, so when after six minutes had passed and she was still screaming, he fought himself and counted another half-minute before opening the door to see her standing up in her crib, hands tugging on the top bar, a big smile coming suddenly when she saw the widening space of light and him standing dumbly in it. And his heart went soft despite the fatigue of his holiday, and he called her "little devil", for she knew all the tricks to melt a father's counting, and not even a year in the world.

He took her onto the big bed and followed her with his hands as she crawled, leaning head-first over the edge. He grabbed her under the arms and lying back tossed her lightly in the air — she left his fingers for less than a second — then caught and lowered her to him slowly with clucking noises and faces that made her laugh. He had shut off the light to relax them, but she was playful in her babbling and spitting raspberries, her reaching out and yanking his nose and beard, knowing that this was a good joke. And so busy in her crawling all over him that he hardly noticed the gentle distending of his body.

Light from the street came through the window. Loose pieces of it that settled on their arms and cheeks as their movements slowed and the nonsense noises of love quietened. When finally she fell asleep beside him, her hand in her mouth, he turned on his side, watching her awhile. In the patches of darkness he was somewhere else, he was half-asleep, gelified and acute as in the tingling numbness of dreams. He leaned over and knew his mouth was opening; a long, deep kiss that pulled at the terry, rough enough so that her hand jerked and she let out a startled cry that made him jump back.

Then pacing beside the big bed, feeling the warm weight of the thing, trying to walk it off like a sleeping foot, looking away, hearing her whine and fuss as if from another room, another house. It's not me, he told himself, it is only love, an adjustment of love. And with deliberate and fierce quickness he picked her up and, holding his arms out in front of him, carried her screaming to the crib.

Rain Wear

I remember those yellow raincoats
and triangle hats, those loud stiff
rinds that never felt like clothing,
more like a cardboard space suit in which
I heard myself move, the patter on my head,
and from which I could see only what
was straight ahead and down.
Like the paper slippers they'd have
in doctors' waiting-rooms,
those stitched-up coffee
filters that made everybody
shuffle with age just to keep them on.

Walking to school inside that tent of
fricatives and hard bends, or watching
a puddle, its soft circles, listening
for Aunt Ruth's station wagon to come
spitting round the corner, and imagining
   Cynthia's kisses — I stood shifting
from foot to foot, a rubber boy
warming to his skin.

repairman to his royal

You're so clean and I'm so happy
I'll get you a new ribbon and we
can dress and undress all day

So what if your step-father finds us
shiny with oil, checks the clock, coughs,
re-doubles his rounds: I just want to play with you,
make you sing a sweet black flower, remnant metal of an
age when our patterings meant something new / 'cause

everything's flying but the question mark's
got to be pulled back by hand and the m is
still mmmmmmmmmm no, it's not stuck anymore
so bolt the door; the boss has gone for the day

and the lover who's been squeezing us with half a
heart, with hems and haws, will tire of our
 simpering, find muscle for the evening
flirt, fuck, and melt to the ground like March snow

While you and I, iron dear
  (in the next room) hunt
and peck each others' i's out
to some blissful-blind counterpoint

2 Down

Saturday Morning

As a child he was Ice-Man, and whatever
he touched turned to crystal.

Or sometimes Fire-Man flicked comets
from his fingertips — bursting lamps, clocks,
bric-a-brac into blazing flower.

Now he's the deadliest hero in the west: Lukewarm Man,
and everything he looks at changes to room
temperature.

Amplitude Modulation

The mayfly lives for just one day
But rock'n'roll is here to stay
Or so the winged humans say
Out of the cradle, endlessly talking

In Moonlight After Rain

— after a scape by F.H. Varley

At the foot of a landscape cleaving
where everything's so darn blue
and aqua and teal and white,
and the tree-thick mountains hang wet,
and the sky, lots of it, seems washed in
quiet affliction —
at the foot of all this
a small figure crossing a bridge,
an earth-clot shadow in a hat.

It is moonlight after rain,
mud and the texture of needles,
the ferrous smell of damp rock
and the human heading bent

toward the middle ground: an island up-cropping
black-green, two tall pines that
spire, lean away from each other like
lovers keeping stubborn silence.

Around, around, around or through?

So much freedom for a shadow!
a blue mountain, a firmament spreading,
a thousand heirs to light and rain,
and that distance into which, when we open
our night eyes, we are always walking

Room Behavior by Rob Kovitz
(cultural studies/architecture/non-fiction)

A woman sits alone in a darkened boiler-room. A man enjoys hanging suspended from the ceiling. A dirty room indicates the secret sexual proclivities of its occupant. A curtain rustling in the breeze portends fear and paranoia.

"The purpose of a room derives from the special nature of a room. A room is inside. This is what people in rooms have to agree on, as differentiated from lawns, meadows, fields, orchards."

Room Behavior is a book about rooms. Composed of texts and images from the most varied sources, including crime novels, decorating manuals, anthropological studies, performance art, crime scene photos, literature, and the Bible, Kovitz shapes the material through a process of highly subjective editing and juxtaposition to create an original, fascinating and darkly funny rumination about the behavior of rooms and the people that they keep.

5 1/2" x 7 1/2" • 288 pages • trade paperback (162 B&W photos) • isbn 1-895837-44-8
Canada $19.99/U.S. $15.99/U.K. £11.99

The War In Heaven by Kent Nussey
The War In Heaven collects the latest work from Kent Nussey. A unique blend of the stark realism of Raymond Carver and the Iyrical precision of Russell Banks, Nussey's writing levels the mythologies of an urban paradise with fictions that are humorous but dark, touching and dangerous. In this book nothing is sacred, secure, or safe. Comprised of seven stories and a novella, *The War in Heaven* explores the human capacity for desire and destruction in a world where everything condenses beyond metaphor into organic connection. For Nussey love is the catalyst, creating the currents which sweep over his complex and provocative characters, and carry the reader to the brink of personal and historical apocalypse.

5 1/4" x 8 1/4" • 192 pages • trade paperback withflaps • isbn 1-895837-42-1
Canada $18.99/U.S. $13.99/U.K. £10.99

Dying for Veronica by Matthew Remski
A love story of bizarre proportions, Matthew Remski's first novel is set in Toronto. *Dying for Veronica* is a gritty and mysterious book, narrated by a man haunted by a twisted and unhappy childhood and obsessed with the sister he loves. This shadowy past explodes into an even more psychologically disturbing present — an irresistible quest

and a longing that can not be denied. Remski's prose is beautiful, provocative, poetic: rich with the dark secrets and intricacies of Catholic mythology as it collides with, and is subsumed by, North American culture.

5 1/4" x 8 1/4" • 224 pages • trade paperback withflaps • isbn 1-895837-40-5
Canada $18.99/U.S. $14.99/U.K. £10.99

Carnival: a Scream In High Park reader edited by Peter McPhee

One evening each July an open-air literary festival is held in Toronto's High Park. It is a midway of diverse voices joined in celebration of poetry and story telling. Audiences exceeding 1,200 people gather under the oak trees to hear both well known and emerging writers from across the country, such as, Lynn Crosbie, Claire Harris, Steven Heighton, Nicole Brossard, Nino Ricci, Al Purdy, Susan Musgrave, Leon Rooke, Christopher Dewdney, Barbara Gowdy, bill bissett... This book collects the work (much of it new and previously unpublished) from the 48 writers who have performed at Scream in High Park in its first three years.

5 1/4" x 8 1/4" • 216 pages • trade paperback withflaps • isbn 1-895837-38-3
Canada $18.99/U.S. $14.99/U.K. £10.99

Beneath the Beauty by Phlip Arima

Beneath the Beauty is Phlip Arima's first collection of poetry. His work is gritty and rhythmic, passionate and uncompromising. His writing reveals themes like love, life on the street and addiction. Arima has a terrifying clarity of vision in his portrayal of contemporary life. Despite the cruelties inflicted and endured by his characters, he is able to find a compassionate element even in the bleakest of circumstances. Arima has a similar aesthetic to Charles Bukowski, but there is a sense of hope and dark romanticism throughout his work. Phlip Arima is a powerful poet and storyteller, and his writing is not for the faint of heart.

5 1/4" x 8 1/4" • 80 pages • trade paperback • isbn 1-895837-36-7
Canada $11.99/U.S. $9.99/U.K. £7.99

What Passes for Love by Stan Rogal

What Passes for Love is a collection of short stories which show the dynamics of male-female relationships. These ten short stories by Stan Rogal resonate with many aspects of the mating rituals of men and women: paranoia, obsession, voyeurism, and assimilation. Stan Rogal's first collection of stories, *What Passes for Love*, is an intriguing search through many relationships, and the emotional turmoil within them. Stan's writing reflects the honesty and unsentimentality, previously seen in his two books of poetry and published stories. Throughout *What Passes for Love* are paintings by Kirsten Johnson.

5 1/4" x 8 1/4" • 144 pages • trade paperback • isbn 1-895837-34-0
Canada $14.99/U.S. $12.99/U.K. £8.99

Bootlegging Apples on the Road to Redemption
by Mary Elizabeth Grace

This is Grace's first collection of poetry. It is an exploration of the collective self, about all of us trying to find peace; this is a collection of poetry about searching for the truth of one's story and how it is never heard or told, only experienced. It is the second story: our attempts with words to express the sounds and images of the soul. Her writing is soulful, intricate and lyrical. The book comes with a companion CD of music/poetry compositions which are included in the book.

5 1/4" x 8 1/4" • 80 pages • trade paperback with cd • isbn 1-895837-30-8
Canada $21.99/U.S. $19.99/U.K. £13.99

The Last Word: an insomniac anthology of canadian poetry
edited by michael holmes

The Last Word is a snapshot of the next generation of Canadian poets, the poets who will be taught in schools — voices reflecting the '90s and a new type of writing sensibility. The anthology brings together 51 poets from across Canada, reaching into different regional, ethnic, sexual and social groups. This varied and volatile collection pushes the notion of an anthology to its limits, like a startling Polaroid. Proceeds from the sale of *The Last Word* will go to Frontier College, in support of literacy programs across Canada.

5 1/4" x 8 1/4" • 168 pages • trade paperback • isbn 1-895837-32-4
Canada $16.99/U.S. $12.99/U.K. £9.99

Desire High Heels Red Wine
Timothy Archer, Sky Gilbert, Sonja Mills and Margaret Webb

Sweet, seductive, dark and illegal; this is *Desire, High Heels, Red Wine*, a collection by four gay and lesbian writers. The writing ranges from the abrasive comedy of Sonja Mills to the lyrical and insightful poetry of Margaret Webb, from the campy dialogue of Sky Gilbert to the finely crafted short stories of Timothy Archer. Their writings depict dark, abrasive places populated by bitch divas, leather clad bodies, and an intuitive sense of sexuality and gender. The writers' works are brought together in an elaborate and striking design by three young designers.

5 1/4" x 8 1/4" • 96 pages • trade paperback • isbn 1-895837-26-X
Canada $12.99/U.S. $9.99/U.K. £7.99

Beds & Shotguns
Diana Fitzgerald Bryden, Paul Howell McCafferty, Tricia Postle & Death Waits
Beds & Shotguns is a metaphor for the extremes of love. It is also a collection by four emerging poets who write about the gamut of experiences between these opposites from romantic to obsessive, fantastic to possessive. These poems and stories capture love in its broadest meanings and are set against a dynamic, lyrical landscape.

5 1/4" x 8 1/4" • 96 pages • trade paperback • isbn 1-895837-28-6
Canada $13.99/U.S. $10.99/U.K. £7.99

Playing in the Asphalt Garden
Phlip Arima, Jill Battson, Tatiana Freire-Lizama and Stan Rogal
This book features new Canadian urban writers, who express the urban experience — not the city of buildings and streets, but as a concentration of human experience, where a rapid and voluminous exchange of ideas, messages, power and beliefs takes place.

5 3/4" x 9" • 128 pages • trade paperback • isbn 1-895837-20-0
Canada $14.99/U.S. $10.99/U.K. £9.99

Mad Angels and Amphetamines
Nik Beat, Mary Elizabeth Grace, Noah Leznoff and Matthew
A collection by four emerging Canadian writers and three graphic designers. In this book, design is an integral part of the prose and poetry. Each writer collaborated with a designer so that the graphic design is an interpretation of the writer's works. Nik Beat's lyrical and unpretentious poetry Noah Leznoff's darkly humorous prose and narrative poetic cycles; Mary Elizabeth Grace's Celtic dialogues and mysti cal images; and Matthew Remski's medieval symbols and surrealistic style of story; this is the mixture of styles that weave together in *Mad Angels and Amphetamines*.

6" x 9" • 96 pages • trade paperback • isbn 1-895837-14-6
Canada $12.95/U.S. $9.95/U.K. £8.99

Insomniac Press • 378 Delaware Ave.
Toronto, Ontario, Canada • M6H 2T8
phone: (416) 536-4308 • fax: (416) 588-4198
email: insomna@pathcom.com